*T*hough I can't **always**
be there with you, Mom...
these words can be.
So I want you to save this
in a **very special** place
and, every now and then,
think of me.

— A. Rogers

Blue Mountain Arts®
Bestselling Titles

By Susan Polis Schutz:
To My Daughter, with Love, on the Important Things in Life
To My Son with Love

By Douglas Pagels:
30 Beautiful Things That Are True About You
42 Gifts I'd Like to Give to You
100 Things to Always Remember... and One Thing to Never Forget
May You Always Have an Angel by Your Side
To the One Person I Consider to Be My Soul Mate

Is It Time to Make a Change?
by Deanna Beisser

I Prayed for You Today
To the Love of My Life
by Donna Fargo

Anthologies:
Always Believe in Yourself and Your Dreams
For You, My Daughter
Friends for Life
Hang In There
I Love You, Mom
I'm Glad You Are My Sister
The Joys and Challenges of Motherhood
The Language of Recovery
Marriage Is a Promise of Love
Teaching and Learning Are Lifelong Journeys
There Is Greatness Within You, My Son
Think Positive Thoughts Every Day
Thoughts to Share with a Wonderful Teenager
True Wealth
With God by Your Side ...You Never Have to Be Alone
You're Just like A Sister to Me

Hugs and Thanks and Lots of Love... for You, MOM

A Very Special Book for My Extraordinary, Fantastic, Irreplaceable Mother

Edited by Diane Mastromarino

Blue Mountain Press ™

Boulder, Colorado

We wish to thank Susan Polis Schutz for permission to reprint the following poems that appear in this publication: "Having a mother like you," "A mother should be," and "You have shown me how to give of myself...." Copyright © 1983, 1984, 1986 by Stephen Schutz and Susan Polis Schutz. All rights reserved.

Library of Congress Control Number: 2005905353
ISBN: 1-59842-113-1

ACKNOWLEDGMENTS appear on page 64.

Certain trademarks are used under license.
BLUE MOUNTAIN PRESS is registered in U.S. Patent and Trademark Office.

Manufactured in the United States of America.
First Printing: 2006

 This book is printed on recycled paper.

This book is printed on fine quality, laid embossed, 80 lb. paper. This paper has been specially produced to be acid free (neutral pH) and contains no groundwood or unbleached pulp. It conforms with the requirements of the American National Standards Institute, Inc., so as to ensure that this book will last and be enjoyed by future generations.

Blue Mountain Arts, Inc.

P.O. Box 4549, Boulder, Colorado 80306

Contents

This is a **very special** book for a mother who has the biggest heart in all the **world**. A mother who loves without condition and never gives up **hope**. A mother who can mend a broken **heart** and chase the clouds away.

This is a book for a mother who is **loved** more than words can express and **appreciated** each and every day by the people lucky enough to know her. A mother who is a **role model**, an adviser, and a friend.

This is a book just for you, **Mom**... the woman who does it all from the person who thinks the **world** of you... **me.**

— Elle Mastro

*y*our heart is **big**. Your love is pure. You want the best for me and care about **everything** I'm going through. You often put my needs above your own and overlook my mistakes. You **love** me without condition. Whatever I am and whatever I do is **okay** with you. You **accept** me... all of me.

You're always there...

...to hear my complaints, to share
my joy, to feel my pain, to listen to
my latest adventure, to advise me,
to cry with me and hope for me and
laugh with me, to forgive me.

Thank you, Mom.

— Donna Fargo

If I could give you the world, I would.
If there were a gift to say
"thank you" for how well you raised me,
I would send it.
But I don't think there could ever be
anything I could give or say
to equal the love and gratitude
I feel for you.

I love you, Mom,
and I carry your **love** in my heart
every day
for **strength** and guidance and courage.
It fills me with **pride** and joy
to have you as my **mother**.

— Cindy Cabral

My Mom

My mom is a person who
   believes in life's bright side.
I know, because she's helped me
   to find it many times.

She is someone who considers
   another's feelings first.
I know, because she's always
   cared for mine.

She is a friend who will stop
   everything else to listen,
to be a special source
   of understanding,
and to offer hope and help
   in any way she can.
I know, because she's always
   been a guiding light for me.

— Barbara J. Hall

In my sky...

There is no light
that shines brighter
that stands so resilient
an inspiration
an enlightening voice
through restless nights
and early mornings
through heartbreak and laughter
smiles and tears
There is nothing so familiar
so comforting, so clear
an eternal promise of love
a source of understanding
and a maker
of wishes come true

...you shine the brightest.

— Deana Marino

You're Such an Amazing Woman...

You **always** seem to accomplish
twice as much as the rest of us,
yet you **always** seem to have
    enough time for all
of life's **important** things.
You do everything possible
    to make your corner of the world
a **beautiful** place to live in.

...and an Even More Amazing Mother

In rushing from one day to the next
and taking care of first things first
in your busy life,
it might be easy to wonder
if anyone else notices the time
you put in
or all the sacrifices you make.
I want you to know that
you really are one of a kind —
and an absolutely awesome mother.

— Jon Peyton

You have handed me **keys** to open the doors of **opportunity**. When one door closes, I have the courage to open another, knowing that no matter what lies behind the door, I have your **love**, **support**, and **friendship** to turn to.

— Sherrilyn Yvonne

You have shown me how to give of myself
You have shown me leadership
You have taught me to be strong
You have taught me the importance of
   the family
You have demonstrated unconditional love
You have demonstrated a sensitivity to
   people's needs
You have handed down to me the important
   values in life
You have handed down to me the idea of
   achieving one's goals
You have set an example, throughout your life
of what a mother and woman should be like

I am so proud of you
and I love you
forever

— Susan Polis Schutz

When I was a child, there was
so much I couldn't understand,
like how hard you worked
and how much you sacrificed
for our family.
There were dreams you had
to put on hold
and dreams that never came true.
You must have felt frustrated
sometimes, no doubt,
and at times even full of despair.
Yet you never gave less
than your best to us.

Every day, you looked after us,
worried about us, fed us,
and **loved us,**
without expecting anything in return.
You see, **Mom,** I know now
and understand
that you actually gave me two lives:
my own... and yours.

— Cheryl Van Gieson

For taking the time...
For all your love...
For being there always...

and promising forever —

Thank you, Mom.

— Elle Mastro

Thank you for taking the hours
out of your own precious days
to make a little more sunlight
    shine in mine.

Thank you...
for being a generous soul
and a beautiful spirit in a world
that could use a million more people
    just like you.

Thanks so much for everything
you've done and for all that you
    continue to do.

— J. Kalispell

This Is Who You Are to Me, Mom

♥ **Y**ou are someone who has **always** been my inspiration... a **precious person** I will always be so grateful for... someone whose wise words have **guided me** through so much.

♥ You are an **angel** who touches my heart more deeply than anyone else... and an **encouraging soul** who lifts me up on the **strength** of her belief in me and on the wings of what she sees in me.

♥ You are a hand holder who **always** shows me the right way to go... a **warm shoulder** who has dried every tear and who chases so many fears away... and the mirror in which I can see reflected all the **good things** about me.

💟 You are a **bridge builder** who helps me rise above just about anything... and a **teacher** whose lessons are with me, in some **meaningful** way, every day.

💟 You are a weaver of **hopes and dreams** who has connected my past with the present and who is so good at picking out the best colors for tomorrow's tapestry... a **nurturing spirit** who has helped me plant the seeds for a more abundant life.

💟 You are my **anchor** and my rock, whom I revere and **respect** and admire enormously... and will forever be the world's **sweetest** and **most special** mother.

— Douglas Pagels

23

Behind the **kindness**
of your smile...

Behind your patience
and **understanding**...

Behind the gentleness
of your **loving heart**...

You tucked away a pair of wings.

(I knew they were there all along, Mom.)

— Maria Michaels

You're My Real-Life Angel

Real-life angels don't hold things against you; the only thing they hold... is you. They take your hand in theirs when you could use a little reassurance. They walk beside you when you could do with a little guidance and direction in your life. And they support you in your attempts to do what is right.

Real-life angels multiply your smiles and add to your integrity. They make you feel like, "Hey, I really am somebody who matters." Then they quietly prove to you how beautiful and true that feeling really is.

♥

— Emilia Larson

If

you hadn't
interfered
and let me know
when I did things
that were
wrong...

If

you had
allowed
me to make
decisions
that I wasn't
old enough to make
on my own...

If
you never
opened your ears
and listened
when I had something
to say…

If
I never
had a mother,
like you,
who cared enough
to set me straight
when I
needed it…

I wouldn't be the person I am today.

— T. L. Nash

5 Things I Learned from You, Mom

I learned that **giving** isn't something we do only in order to receive. We give to **help** those who need it and to show those closest to us how much we **care**.

I learned that **dreams** are precious, and although we all have them, each one is **unique**.

I learned that **success** is not measured by dollars or possessions. Success is **following your heart** and doing the things that make you **happy**.

I learned that bad times don't last **forever**. Whether facing an obstacle or overcoming grief, hard times do pass. When there is a cloudy sky, the **sun** is not gone. It is only hidden for a while.

I learned that no matter what **silly** thing I may have said or done, a **mother's love** is and will always be **unconditional**.

— April Aragam

Though no one person
may be able to change
the world...
you have made
a significant difference
in my life,
and I appreciate you.

— Grace F. Dement

You Work So Hard and Do So Much

Day in and day out, you make the world a better place to be. And the people who are **lucky** enough to be in your life are the ones who get to see that you're a very **wonderful** person with a **truly** gifted touch. You go a million miles out of your way and you **always** do so much... to make sure that others' lives are easier and filled with **happiness**. Your caring could never be taken for granted because the people you're close to are **blessed**... with someone who works at a job well-done to bring **smiles** to the day.

— Jenn Davids

Moms are **teachers**, dreamers, hopers, believers, **coaches**, leaders, finders, seekers, **growers**, bakers, movers, shakers, followers, **seers**, and keepers.

Moms are encouragers,
helpers and **speakers**,
storytellers, excellent spellers,
amazing women,
and **friends**.

— Ashley Rice

*B*eing a mother
   is a **full-time** job.
It requires the stamina
   of an Olympic athlete,
the **talents** of a
   master teacher,
the **devotion** of a missionary, and
   the skills of a "Jill-of-all-trades."
It tests patience, **self-control,**
   and sanity.

A mother knows
  all the answers to things
like "Why is the sky blue?"
  and "Where do babies come from?"
She teaches numbers and colors
  and shapes
and what not to say
  when visitors come.
A mother's heart swells with
  overwhelming love
because being a mother is
  the greatest job
    in the world.

— Jacqueline Schiff

$\mathcal{H}$aving a **mother** like you
makes it easy to grow up
into a loving, strong adult

— Susan Polis Schutz

Εvery day,
I thank you silently for the wisdom
you have imparted to me.
I thank you for the values that you
instilled in me.
But most of all, I thank you
for loving me so much
that I can still feel it
deep within my heart.

— Lea Walsh

*Y*ou were **always** the one who listened when I spoke and who chose to be with me when the rest of the world moved on. You were the one who **cared** how I felt and **encouraged** my wildest dreams. You didn't expect perfection in me, but accepted my worst faults. You held my hand and **comforted** my deepest pains. When I felt alone, you stayed beside me, a **constant source** of hope to guide me.

You allowed me to **be myself** and to be true to my inner voice, even when the real me wasn't who you would have liked me to be. You **understood** my silence, and when I was quiet, you allowed me the space I needed for thought. You showed me what it means to feel loved unconditionally, **without limitations** or expectations. You were always there, available to share whatever came my way. Without you, I don't know where I might be.

— Regina Hill

You've taught me
that an open **heart**
moves mountains
and that **great** things
come to those who **love**.

You've shown me
that **happiness** means
being yourself.

You've taught me
that being **thoughtful**
is more important
than being thought of.

You've shared your
talents with me
and helped me to
develop **my own.**

You've gotten me
started on the right foot
and **picked me up**
when I stumbled.

You've helped me
understand that the
biggest mistakes can
lead to the **greatest** rewards.

— Kari Kampakis

A Little Math for Mom

Think of something you couldn't
   live without...
and **multiply** it by a hundred.

Think of what happiness
   means to you...
and **add** it to the feelings you get
on the best days you've ever had.

Add up all your best feelings
and take away all the rest...
and what you're left with is
exactly how I feel about you.

— Alin Austin

How Do You Thank Someone for the Moon and Stars?

I could spend a lifetime searching for the **right words** to say to you. The perfect words would be filled with **appreciation** for someone who took me by the hand when I was little and who **guided me** on a pathway toward more **happiness** than most people will ever know.

The right words would tell you
how **dear** you will always be to
me for **holding** the ladders that
reached to my own little stars, for
catching me whenever I fell,
and for always being there with
encouragement, support,
and **understanding.**

— Laurel Atherton

I love you as my mom,
but most of all...

as my friend.

— Cheryl Gray

If you weren't my mother, I'd choose you for **my friend**. You've always accepted me **wholeheartedly** and unconditionally, and that means **everything** to me.

Like a caring angel, you've **sheltered** me and **carried** me on your wings. You've stood by my side when I needed you to, and you've been **patient** as I've learned my own lessons. You've taught by example that love and family are the most **important** things in life.

— Donna Fargo

There is something about **family**
 that is so strong —
it's stronger than words,
 stronger than friendship,
stronger than anything else
 in the **world.**

Family is a feeling of **forever**
without having to say the words.
It's a feeling of **love**
without needing to explain why.
It lives in the **deepest** places
 of the heart —
where memories are kept,
where **laughter** is free and easy,
where promises are unspoken
 and **never** broken.

With you, there will always be a place
where I'll feel right at home.
We have a connection between us
that nothing can ever change.
I love you because we're family...
but also just because you're you, Mom,
someone wonderful
who will always be held in
the deepest part of my heart.

— Carol Thomas

The bond between us
is ENORMOUS...
and though sometimes it's not
perfect, it's something I can
always count on when it feels as if
everything else is falling apart.

— Pamela Malone-Melton

You held my hand when I was afraid
and helped me to mend
my first broken heart.
You bandaged my wounds,
wiped my tears,
and kept me from falling apart.

You loved me without question,
no matter what I did.
You shaped me into
a confident adult
from such an awkward kid.

Even though you're not always
right beside me,
your love is matched by
no other.
And I thank God each day
for His greatest gift:
making you my mother.

— Stacey Swayze

Time and time again, you remind me
what the power of a mother's love
   can do.
You've seen the "real me,"
and yet somehow still think
   of me as someone special;
you've known me at my worst,
and yet your caring never loses
   any of its strength.
It's so amazing to have a mom
   like you.

You have the **ability** to put yourself
    in my shoes
even if it's a tight squeeze,
and you have the know-how
to keep me pointed in the **right direction**.
There's a **special** tie between us
that grows more beautiful
    through the years —
with **memories**, like ribbons,
that will forever keep us close at **heart**.

— Linda E. Knight

These Are the Gifts
I Would Like to Give to You

A heartfelt thank-you... for all the things you do for me ✎ My **assurance**... that I **really** <u>do</u> remember the things you taught me, and I **always** will ✎ **Plenty** of reasons... for you to feel **proud** of me, which I'll achieve by **always** striving to be and do my best ✎ A **sincere** apology... for **any** headaches I may have caused you when I was growing up ✎

A **gift certificate**... to be redeemed anytime — as many times as you want — for **anything** I can ever do for you ✎ My **promise**... that no matter how far away from home I may travel, you are **never** far from my heart ✎

My continued **commitment**... to our family and the values you have taught me ✎ **Recognition**... for all the **great** things you've done in your life (not the least of which was me!) ✎ An **invitation**... to **always** be a part of my life, and to never feel that you have to ask ✎ A bunch of **wishes**... that you have peace, joy, and happiness in your life, which you are so deserving of ✎ My **love**... forever and **always** ✎

— Anna Marie Edwards

For the 1,000,000,000,000,000,000 Times You've Been on My Side

I couldn't begin
to count
the number of times
you **tolerated** my moods,
consoled my heartbreaks
   and disappointments,
endured my ups and downs,
listened to words
confused by tears,
and just simply
understood...

for no other reason
than because
you love me.

— Susan M. Pavlis

$\mathcal{A}$ mother should be
strong and guiding
understanding and giving
A mother should be
honest and forthright
confident and able
A mother should be
relaxed and soft
flexible and tolerant
But most of all
a mother should be a
loving woman
who is always there when needed

Mom, you are a rare
and wonderful woman
You are everything
that a mother should be
and more

— Susan Polis Schutz

There have been **many** times when
 I have missed the chance to tell you
 that I'm so **proud** of you and all
 you stand for.
I **respect** your discipline, your
 decisions, and the way you **stand**
 by your words.
I **admire** everything about your way
 of life, even though you may have
 wondered many times if I was even
 listening when you **spoke** to me.

You may have **felt** as if your words
were falling on closed ears, but
I've **always** heard you.
It is those messages of yours that
have **helped** me, guided me,
and kept me **safely** going on.

— Barbara J. Hall

A Great Big Thank-You to You, Mom!

With the **deepest** kind of gratitude
and the **sweetest** kind of joy,

I simply want to thank you for being...

all that you are to me.

— Douglas Pagels

*Y*our love has **always** been
the most constant thing
   in my **life**.
From the time I was born,
you have been there for me —
     my source of **warmth** and **comfort**,
     my **greatest** encouragement,
     my **biggest** fan,
     my confidante,
     my best and truest **friend**...
      my **precious** mom.

For all that you are,
for all that you do,
for all your love,
I thank you with all my heart.

— Helen Vincent

ACKNOWLEDGMENTS

We gratefully acknowledge the permission granted by the following authors and authors' representatives to reprint poems or excerpts from their publications.

PrimaDonna Entertainment Corp. for "Your heart is big..." and "If you weren't my mother..." by Donna Fargo. Copyright © 1998, 2006 by PrimaDonna Entertainment Corp. All rights reserved.

April Aragam for "5 Things I Learned from You, Mom." Copyright © 2006 by April Aragam. All rights reserved.

Jacqueline Schiff for "Being a mother is a full-time job." Copyright © 2006 by Jacqueline Schiff. All rights reserved.

Regina Hill for "You were always the one who listened...." Copyright © 2006 by Regina Hill. All rights reserved.

Kari Kampakis for "You've taught me that an open heart...." Copyright © 2006 by Kari Kampakis. All rights reserved.

A careful effort has been made to trace the ownership of selections used in this anthology in order to obtain permission to reprint copyrighted material and give proper credit to the copyright owners. If any error or omission has occurred, it is completely inadvertent, and we would like to make corrections in future editions provided that written notification is made to the publisher:

BLUE MOUNTAIN ARTS, INC., P.O. Box 4549, Boulder, Colorado 80306.